When A Man Cries

HEATHER GROSS

Tellwell Talent
www.tellwell.ca

ISBN
978-0-2288-7120-0 (Hardcover)
978-0-2288-7121-7 (Paperback)

DEDICATION

I would like to say that this book is Holy Spirit inspired. I would like to thank God for giving me this book to write for Him. I would also like to thank my mom and dad for input and feedback to help me in the writing process of this book.

TABLE OF CONTENTS

CHAPTER 1

The Heart of Man

This book contains some prophetic words and was directly written for husbands that are struggling in their marriage. This book is reminders of God's love for husbands and a guide for them to full-fill their roles as husbands as God intended so that they may have the abundant life he promised.

God says the heart accommodates the spirit of man. What this means is that when you receive the spirit of the living God, also known as the Holy Spirit, the Holy Spirit He teaches the spirit of man to be like your Father God to understand your Father. The Holy Spirit is your helper within you, who is your friend who guides you into all that your Father has called you to be. Everyone that is born has their own spirit within them; this is known as the spirit man. The Holy Spirit helps change the things that need to change within your spirit man in order for you to be in His likeness.

Some men portray themselves a certain way hiding what is underneath the surface. Men are not showing that they have vulnerabilities. Some men put up their defenses afraid that they will appear or seem weak if others know how they truly feel or think.

The heart is a spiritual organ that drives men's behavior. The heart decides their thoughts and behavior. What is in their heart is going to reflect how they behave and what they decide to do in their actions. God says "Receding is the heart of man as he complies with the ways of this world." Men choose to follow the ways of the world over the ways of God. This causes a separation between men and God.

God says "Concubine of the heart." Man's heart is not faithful to God because he fills himself with other desires and idols. This does not allow room for God to work in him and his heart. God says "Prevention of the heart." What that means is stopping the ways of the world from coming in your heart. Allow the things of God to flow in your heart doing the things of God. You have to choose to put the things of God over the things of this world and live according to the ways of God over the things of the world.

God says "Agriculture of the heart." This means that you have to water and nurture the heart and love it with the things of God. The way to love your heart with the things of God is to fill yourself with his Word take the time to have conversation with God. Praise and worship Him for all that He does in your life. Also spend time with others and share in the love that you have for God and also the love that God has shared with you.

God says "Recirculating the heart." This means getting into the Word of God letting it change your heart. When you allow the Word of God to be embedded in your heart you meditate and live according to God's Word. When you live by it than your heart will begin to change. Suddenly your heart will thirst for the things of God and not the things of this world. You will begin to desire the things of God in your heart.

God says "The heart must be like a butterfly exploring the things of God." God wants you to know about all the things that are of Him. It makes God happy for you to want to learn about Him. God is where your identity should be rooted. You should want to learn and grow in him and all that is him. To understand and know who God is will help you to understand and know who you are because you are His child who He loves.

God says "Picking the knees over the things of the world." It means surrendering to the things of God over the things of the world. To fall on your knees is to surrender to God and not choose the things of the world knowing that God is the one in control of all things. And it also means trusting and believing God will be there for you in your time of need when you feel that nobody else is.

God says "Profiteering is the heart of man excluding me as I call out to them." Man chooses to put his priority on profits and exclude God even though He is calling out to them. When man's heart and attention are focused on the profits he can obtain he does not include God in his plans. God wants to be included in your plans and He should be your priority. He can make all of your paths straight if you would just let Him. God is calling out to you trying to get you to listen but you have to be willing and understand how much God truly loves and wants what is best for you.

God says "In exclusion have they been routing their way through life." Man has been excluding God and trying to live his own way. Man goes and does what he wants to do. He thinks that he knows what is best for him and does not feel the need for God.

God says "Condescending are the thoughts of man." This mentality is a sense of superiority that takes away from God's glory. As children of the most high King we should recognize that no one is above anyone. Everyone is equal and should be helping one another showing all that God shows to you to others.

God says "Unsettling are the thoughts of man." What this means is that man's thoughts are not right with God. Man allows his thoughts to be filled with the things of the world and not the things of God. Man's thoughts should be focused on God our Creator. If you are not thinking of

Him and building that relationship with Him than we can't understand and know who we are in Him.

God says "The heart of man is wild and untamed." This means that man is not letting God rule his heart but allowing the world to rule his heart and his desires. He is putting things of the world over God and this is what makes the heart untamed. The things of the world will never satisfy man's heart because God is the only one who can make man's heart feel complete. The empty void that man feels in his heart was always meant to be filled with God, not other things.

God says "Unwilling is man to understand the power of the living God." Man refuses to believe God has the ultimate power over all things. Man thinks he is in control of his life and all things, but that couldn't be further from the truth. God controls all things whether man thinks so or not. When man feels there is no way to overcome something or things can't get any better, he is wrong. Through every circumstance and every situation God can make a way when there is no way. There is nothing that God can't do; He has no limitations.

God says "Accusations of me resentments of me is their hearts towards me." Man chooses to blame God for all that is unpleasant in his life. It is easier to blame than to accept he is accountable for his choices and for the way he lives out his life. God is not behind things that happen to us in fact he is the one who takes the bad things that happen to us and turn it into something good. He takes what the enemy meant for evil and turns it for good. He takes circumstances and situations and makes them meaningful and useful for His purpose.

God says "Reluctant are their ways." Man is not very straightforward in his ways. Man tends to do things with hesitation instead of being clear about motives and intentions and how he feels. God however can help man to be straightforward because He is a God of Truth and He is also a God who is relentless and knows exactly what to do and how to handle whatever you may face. God says "Heart of man is not of one mind according to God." The heart of man wants many things and is not devoted to having his heart and mind set on God. Man is not set on just having one particular thing but wants many things and those many things are not focused on God. Instead the focus is on his desires, thoughts, motives and all that he wants instead of what God wants. When man sets his heart and mind on the things of God than his life will begin to change for the better in an abundance of all God has for him.

God says "Rebuttal is the heart of man excluding re-engaging with the ways of the world." This means man's heart is against God excluding Him and re-engaging in the ways of the world. It means having known God and choosing to leave Him out and choose the ways of the world over Him. Man's heart opposes the ways of God, but the ways of God will not cause the pain and suffering that the ways of the world causes. And when you have a relationship with God, even if you suffer and are challenged, God will always help you to overcome and face whatever it is.

God says "Precarious are the hearts of man." What this means is that man's heart is unpredictable. Man's heart is impulsive. God wants man's heart to be faithful and to stay grounded in Him and nothing else. God says "They see what they want to see but not that of God." Man is focused on his own desires and things that he wants. He is not considerate or thoughtful about the things of God. When you focus on God and what He wants for you it does not compare to the things that you want or desire for yourself.

God says "Seeing all they want to see but not caring about the things of God." Man only has the perception of the things that matter to him but not regarding the things of God. Man's heart has become hardened and doesn't allow for the things of God to come into his heart.

God says "Dulled in vision and separated from the things of God." Man is busy living of the world and living in sin, separating himself from God. When you put your vision on God, your life becomes more than you could ever imagine. You realize how much more you can do and be and have with God. When you fully depend on Him you can rest assured He will always be there for you.

God says "Reducing their hearts to the world." All man's vision, heart, and everything is set on the world and not God and what He has for him. Man needs less of himself and more of God. God says "Their eyes do not see their hearts do not cry out not looking for me." Man is too blinded in the heart and the mind to see God. Man thinks he can get through life all by himself and feels he has no need for God. The truth is you need God for everything. He can improve everything you do in abundance. If man cries out to Him and asks for help, He will always help his children.

God says "Relinquishing their selves of me." Man has let themselves go of anything having to do with God. Everything that man has is because of God. God wants man to know Him and know His love. He loves man so much that He gave His one and only son Jesus to die for our sins so that we would be able to have a relationship with Him.

God says "Their hearts are far from me."Man is not concerned with the price that Jesus paid for all of us to live free of sin. Also man does not take into account what a sacrifice it was for God to sacrifice His one and only son for all of us because He loved us that much. God says "The heart of man is quenched from the things of God." The love man used to have for God has been put out. Man's heart is so filled with the things of this world that it doesn't allow room for God and the things of God. Man has to allow himself to open his heart so that God can work in him and through him, changing his life.

God says "Man must learn to allow God to come in and relite the heart." Man has to allow God to change the heart so he can be set on fire for Him. To allow God to change your heart means that you have to be willing to accept change. Man has to be willing to turn away from his ways and learn to live and walk in God's ways. God's ways are not man's ways but his ways are better ways of living.

God says "The reasoning's of the heart of man will it not bring calamity if not changed." Man has to change his reasoning to the ways of God so that he will not have calamity. If man chooses to act and think his way it will bring calamity. Calamity is separation from God. If man wants to know and understand God's reasoning he can read the Word of God. Man does not understand separation from God is the worst thing that can happen to somebody. The closer you are to God the better your life will be regardless of what challenges you may face. The further you are from God the harder your life will be. God wants to make man's life better but he has to allow himself to submit to Him. For man to reach his full potential, he has to give up his ways and all the things that he puts as priority over God.

God says "Unattainable is the heart of man if they don't open the door unto me." Man has to open his heart to God because if he doesn't than the heart is unattainable. Man has to be willing and open to let God mold and shape him to be in His likeness.

God says "Man has a barbed wire fence around his heart trying to hold back from receiving the things of God. But

I tell you this I will begin to clip the fence. Ongoing is the hand of God that will remove all that is against me." Man has defenses built up around his heart refusing to allow anyone or anything in. These built up defenses that man has around his heart causes him to not be able to receive the things of God. The hand of God is always moving and He will clip the barbed wire around man's heart to get rid of the things that are against him. More than anything God wants man's heart. The heart is what acknowledges and accepts and loves God.

God says "Public enemy #1 is your own heart." You cannot trust your heart because it is full of evil, and all things of the world, and not of God. God says "He wants our hearts to establish and fix them in accordance in His ways." God is the fixer of your heart and He wants to fix your heart but He wants your heart in accordance with His ways and the way He created you to be. God didn't make your heart for the ways of the world. He made your heart for the things of God. He made your heart for Him to be the ruler of your heart. God wants for you to know Him and walk in His ways. God wants what any good father wants for His children, His children to be in His likeness.

God says "Unchanging is the heart unless you allow God to do his work." Man has to be willing and open to change in order for God to do His work in your heart. The way that God looks at you is not how you perceive yourself. Some of the things you may see as acceptable God may see as things that need to change. Also something's you may think need to change He may see as something that will help you become all He has called you to be.

God says "By standards the heart is the greatest way to acknowledge God." What this means is to give your all and everything to God in order to acknowledge Him. Man has to be willing to give every single part of himself and to surrender to God. Doing this acknowledges God in the heart. It is fully understanding that everything belongs to God and He is the one who can fix and change the things that are not of Him in your life. God says "Your heart is either a temple of God or a habitation of Satan." Depending of what you have in your heart, by your behavior and choices you are either serving God or you are serving Satan.

God says "Reclaiming the heart is of me. Surrendering the heart is of you." God is the owner of your heart and He is the only one to fix and mend your heart and what is wrong with it. God is not going to force you to love Him. It is your choice how much. You have to allow Him to come in your heart and work in your life.

God says "Be it of me that I call out to them that would not listen." God calls out to the people who don't listen. His love is so unconditional for everyone. God doesn't want a single person to be lost. He wants to save everybody. 2 Peter 3:9: "The Lord is not slow in keeping his promise, as some understand slowness. Instead he is patient with you, not wanting anyone to perish, but everyone to come to repentance."

Jesus said "I have come that they would know me and my Father." Jesus has come so that everyone would know Him and His Father. Jesus and his father are one to know and understand Jesus is to know and understand the Father.

God says "Where is the heart that I created to observe Me, to love Me, to live with Me?" God created all of man to observe Him, to love Him, and to live with Him. There is no comparison for how much He loves you but you have allowed other things to get in your mind and heart instead of God.

God says "The heart have I not seen." God has not seen man's heart dedicated to Him even though man's heart belongs to God.

God says "The hearts that seclude themselves far from me." Man hides himself from God but He knows all things and sees all things. There is nothing that God cannot do or accomplish. He is the ruler over all things and has no limitations or boundaries.

God says "Oh the time is coming that all will know Me, believing in Me and knowing Me is there such a time as this that man would fall to their knees cry out to Me." Man will know God and who He is. God wants you to know that He is here for you and all you go through.

God says "Oh that they would hear Me and understand Me." God wants you to hear Him and understand Him.

God says "Hear when I say my love cries out that every ear would hear." God loves you so much His love cries out for you to hear Him and know Him. God has love for you.

God says "Exonerate the heart." What that means is God will free your heart of other things. God says "As the sea crushes its waves against the rocks so am I towards the heart of man. Relentless am I conquering the heart." God has so much love for you and He will fight for you. He will not give up on you and is determined to win over your heart. God says "I am he who knocks at the door of the Heart and He says let me come in allow Me to change your heart because I won't force My way. I call out to man that they would hear Me." God wants to be invited into your heart to change your heart and make you better. He wants you to hear Him. He doesn't force himself on you; you have to make a choice to want to know Him better and allow Him to change you and change your life.

A pure heart for God means that the person has no desire to sin whatsoever. They want to be aligned with God's will in all aspects. Their desire is to only think and do those things that are pleasing to God. That is how all of us should be striving to be for God. God says "I will change the disturbances in the heart of man." What this means is God will change all the things in men's heart that keeps him separated from him. An example would be lust. God can change these desires in your heart to strive to want the things of God.

CHAPTER 2

Challenges of Man

What does forbearance mean? It means patience, self-control and tolerance. Forbearance is what men should exemplify. An example of forbearance would be in all aspects of life he shows patience to his wife, his children, and everyone that he encounters. He also should show self-control. There will be people who are not the easiest to deal with and this is when he should put into practice self-control. He should always remember that he is exemplifying to his wife, his children, and also other followers of Jesus. The last way he should be an example to others is show tolerance. He should show tolerance to others in order to show that he has the love of Jesus in him and others can see and come to know Jesus. If he is lacking any of these things, he should pray for God to supply what he does not have. God will give you all that you need if you ask for it. God says "Striving with anticipation to please your Father. Cooperation with the Father brings forth life." It should be your goal not only to be an example of Him but also for you to be working towards doing what is pleasing to Him. Working with the Father allows you to walk in the purpose that He has given you.

God says "Be patient, slow to anger, and steadfast love not to be scrutinizing." You should be patient in order to help prevent conflict but also to show others the ways of God. Man should be slow to anger so that it does not create more turmoil with others as well as to walk in the ways of God. Last of all man should show steadfast love. This is very important because to know God is to know love because God is love. His love is steadfast which means it is unmovable and will not change. This is the same kind of love that man should be showing to others. Man should not have love that sways or is showing any kind of favoritism because God has unchanging love for everyone.

Man also should not be scrutinizing to others. He should be kind and accepting and always know that God made each one of us different and for a specific purpose that He has planned. Man should not be criticizing or judging anyone closely because that is not showing the love of God.

A husband should love God more than he loves his wife. He cannot make his wife an idol that is a sin. Nothing should come before God; He should always be one's first priority. Man should fear God more than he fears his wife. In a marriage God should be number one and the spouse should be number two. When God becomes both spouses first priority, He will work in both husband and wife to show his attributes between both of them. If the husband or wife is not putting God first it will cause an imbalance and create marital problems. God has to be at the center of the marriage in order for it to blossom and grow. He will nurture and take care of both spouses allowing His love to grow between the both of you and to expand so much that it also pours out to others.

A husband is the spiritual leader in the marriage. He should lead his wife into doing the things of God such as ministry, devotionals, praying, reading and learning the word of God, and also worship. The husband is the one who should be pushing his wife to grow closer and closer to God. He should take the lead in initiating the things of God with his wife. The wife is the one who follows after the husband so what the husband does the wife will also do. It's very important that the husband is a good example to his wife in order for her to have a close relationship with God, and so she can begin accomplishing the goals and plans that God has for her and her life.

Husbands are supposed to be able to lead with humility. Men's leadership should be putting others before yourself. Husbands should have Christ like qualities. Not only does having Christ like qualities show an example to your wife but it also shows an example to others on how they should also be. It's very important to show humility because God does not like pridefulness or arrogance. Being prideful or arrogant can cause problems and it is not showing the qualities of Jesus.

Husbands should have godly courage. They should have a fear of God over anything else. If a man is not of Godly courage, he should ask for godly courage. It is important that a husband has Godly courage so that he may encourage his wife to seek God before all things. A husband having godly courage helps boost your wife's faith in God when unexpected challenges happen. If a husband does not have godly courage, this can create problems of fear and not knowing or realizing the power of God in stressful situations. A husband should not allow fear to creep in. "For God has not given us a spirit of fear, but of power and of love and of sound mind" (2 Timothy 1:7)

It is the husband's job to be a provider. The husband carries the responsibility for his household. A provider is someone who expects situations and does the decisive planning for the household. He is supposed to think about the goals, not just finances but spiritual goals and emotional goals. The husband guides the direction of his wife with the help of God. It is the husband's responsibility for he is leading his wife in her life and the way that he supports her.

Husbands are to love your wives biblically and extravagantly placing your wives needs above your own. Sacrifice for your wife even when you don't see eye to eye. She should be your priority. After your love for God love your wife more than anything else in the world. A husband should want to go above and beyond for his wife to love her and to make her happy. More than anything as husband honor your wife by the way you treat her, talk to her and by the things you do for her. You should treat your wife how God treats your wife and nothing less than that.

Honor your wife amongst the congregation to be the example of how the husbands should treat their wives in the congregation. If you are not honoring your wife amongst the congregation you are setting a bad example to them. Not only are you setting a bad example but you are showing them that you are not putting God first by honoring your wife. Prayers will be hindered if you do not honor your wife. Treat her right and have respect for her. God wants you to treat your wife as valuable and take care of her and treat her the way that He treats her. You should treat your wife with kindness, compassion, understanding, patience and unconditional love just as God does.

Men struggle with concerns of their children growing up and living for Jesus as adults. Men also have the pressure of making sure to be an example and role model. Men should always be praying for their children but also showing through example how their children should live in order to influence their children and show how they should be. Men should be leaning on Jesus to understand His ways, to walk in His ways, and to be able to teach their children how to understand and walk in His ways. It's very important that man is seeking a close relationship with God in order to teach his children how to have a close relationship with God.

Men struggle with settling for the wrong kinds of friends. Men choose friends who are fun to be around but that they can be led astray into worldly things. When men choose these kinds of friends, they are not getting the prayer and support they need. Also men should be seeking friends who are men of God and will push them and cause them to grow closer to God. Men should not affiliate with worldly friends unless they are giving testimony to them. It is easier for someone on the right path to be led astray than to influence someone on the wrong path.

Some men don't want to face their problems inside themselves or take honest responsibility. They may be afraid to share what is going on with them with other men. More men need to learn to be like Jesus He expressed all His emotions. Some men have a hard time expressing how they feel inside for the fear of how they will be seen if they show it. An example is crying: some men feel too vulnerable in crying and would rather keep those feelings inside than express it. Some men feel that crying makes them inferior but that is not the truth. More men should express all their feelings being truthful and honest about what they are feeling inside. More men should be bolder like Jesus, to have courage no matter the situation because they know God is with them always.

Some men have the problem of putting the woman in their life as their only friend. It is unhealthy to put all your burdens onto one person and to ask them to make you accountable. This kind of relationship can be damaging to the woman for carrying too much of the man's baggage. God is the one that you come to with your burdens and others help you to feel supported and to know you can overcome with God's help and guidance. It can help a man to have close male friends who have a relationship with Jesus for things that a woman cannot understand. Another man can understand the temptations, the struggles and pressures of life, and how to be a godly man. It's not about being open and honest with other men; you need men who will push you to become a stronger disciple. Also it's significant that you push other men too. Don't just dwell and speak of your challenges but push yourself to overcome them with the help of Jesus and encourage others to do the same.

Some men struggle with the temptation of worshiping their work. God put it in man to want to work and a man working is for God's glory. It's okay for a man to like working but it's not okay for a man to worship his work. Worshiping work is bowing down to your work as priority instead of God and your family. God should always be your very first priority and you should ask for help and guidance when you struggle with certain challenges at work. Work will not give you all that God can provide and give you. You may enjoy the benefits of work for a while but the benefits of what God will give to you will endure. "Whatever you do, work at it with all your heart, as working for the Lord not for human masters," (Col 3:23) you are not working for people but you are working for God and he is where you will find your purpose and fulfillment.

Another obstacle some men struggle with at work is time. You are not taking the time at work to speak to God. You also are not making the time to worship and praise Him. You have children, and wives, and are the leaders in the family to set an example but God has to be the one you put as priority to handle your time and all the things that you face. When you put God first, He allows all things to come into place for you.

One of the challenges some men struggle with are temptations at work. The challenges that they face are challenges of engaging in doing things not of God. Men have the temptation to choose be dishonest at work for their own gain. They also have to deal with ungodliness at work and making the decision to not engage in ungodly behavior. Some examples of ungodly behaviors at work are: slander, rumors, and profanity. When you partake in doing these things it is not serving God. When you are at work you should show your godly values over the values of the world that may be surrounding you. If you are tempted to do something that you shouldn't do pray about it because God will not allow temptation beyond what you can handle. It is completely up to you if you do something or not, but God wants the best for you and for you to make better choices.

Jesus is your boss. Remember when you have work problems to pray to God. Jesus is the one you actually work for and you should reflect His attributes to others at work such as kindness, patience, forbearance, and humility. When you show the attributes of God it causes others to be drawn toward Him and to want to get to know Him. More men should be doing all they can to show Jesus's qualities so that others will want to be led to Him. The priority of work is to shine Jesus's light through you so that others will want to come to know Him and when they receive Him, they will also become children of God.

God works in you through your work. Many people without even knowing each other work together in God's work in providing for one another. Even the smallest gesture or minor act of kindness is God working through you. Everyone is connected to each other and when someone does something for someone else that is God providing and making a way for something to happen for them. God has chosen you to work through you, your abilities, and your knowledge for the good of others. God is living in you and molding and shaping you to do exactly what it is He wants you to do in order to be able to reach others.

You can lean on God with your profession. Jesus has set you free from all anxiety. You can trust God completely to supply your every need. What you are lacking He will supply you with. He will meet you in the middle of everything and help you to endure and work through you despite what is going on around you. God takes circumstances and he makes them beneficial for his purpose. You don't have to worry about things going wrong because what started out as bad can be meant for something good. God has plans to prosper you, to give you a hope and a future. When you are having problems or struggles and feel you can't deal with what you are going through, call on Him and He will answer. He will give you more than enough of whatever you are asking. He is always with you and for you and will give you exactly what you need.

Some men have challenges with temptation. One of the temptations some men deal with is taking the easy way out to get success. There is no bypass to the will of God on your life. You try to use get rich quick mind set to your walk with God and it does not work. God doesn't want you to try to take the easy way out. Sometimes the harder way and challenges you face teach you what you need to understand and know. Everything that God allows to happen is for a reason, whether you understand or not.

God expects an attitude of gratitude, not to behave like you are owed something from Him. Always be careful to be modest as God lifts you up. If you don't do this than you could have your blessing come to a complete halt if you allow pride to creep in. You should have no sense of entitlement, because God is always working on your behalf and you should always remain thankful for each and everything that He does for you.

You can't live a Christian life on the outside and nurture a life completely the opposite on the inside. This hypocrisy will create a spiritual disturbance that will slowly separate you away from God. The heart is valuable to God, not how you appear to others. Your mind should be in submission to God. You should make sure that how you are on the inside reflects how you are on the outside. Both inside and outside should reflect God and who He is and all His ways by the way you live.

Another temptation that some men face in society is sexual impurity. You find it in television, books, magazines, and also sexual temptation can be right in front of you. Sexual temptation can't be avoided because it's everywhere. It's up to you to put the values of God over the temptations of the world. If you resist temptation the devil will flee. God does not allow temptation beyond what you can handle.

Some men struggle with the temptation of choosing idols over God. These idols that some men struggle with are power, status, accomplishment, and reputation. You are to put others before yourselves and not be self- seeking. You should be aiming towards the goals and the plans that God has for you and helping and striving to expand the kingdom of God. Jesus made Himself nothing and a servant to man, you are to have that same attitude to glorify him. When you choose these idols over God's will then you allow yourself to be used by the devil.

Some men struggle with the temptation of choosing money over everything. Money is their idol. They may have the mindset of trying to earn more money to get more things. More things will not fulfill them; there is only one thing that can completely fulfill them and that is God. God is the only one that has an abundance of all that you need. Some men are missing that alone time with God and also time with their family because they are putting money as priority over everything. The love of money is the root of all evil. "For the love of money is a root of all kinds of evil. Some people, eager for money, have wandered from the faith and pierced themselves with many grief's." (1 Tim 6:10)

Some men struggle with one last temptation: becoming too involved in the things of the world that they neglect their spiritual life and growing closer to God. More men need to stand strong in knowing who God is and what He can do to build them up in the spirit. When you grow closer to God you also grow spiritually, enabling you to become who you are in Jesus. Allowing yourself to grow spiritually by growing close to God will prepare you to endure whatever attacks may come. More men need to make God a priority and take that time to be alone with Him, getting to know Him and His ways so that others may come to know Him also. Spending time alone with God will cause you to grow spiritually and allow you to become who He has called you to be in Him.

CHAPTER 3

Threshing Floor

What is the threshing floor? The threshing floor is referred to biblically as a symbol of judgment. John the Baptist used the visual of the threshing floor to describe that Jesus is to come and will separate the true believers from the fake. The actual believers of Christ will be brought together into the kingdom of God but the ones who reject Jesus will be burned up with a fire that won't go out.

An example image of the threshing floor is the Parable of The Wheat and Tares.

(Matt 13:36-43) "Then He left the crowd and went into the house. His disciples came to Him and said, "Explain to us the parable of the weeds in the field." He answered, "The one who sowed the good seed is the Son of Man. The field is the world, and the good seed stands for the people of the kingdom. The weeds are the people of the evil one, and the enemy who sows them is the devil.

The harvest is the end of the age, and the harvesters are angels. "As the weeds are pulled up and burned in the fire, so it will be at the end of the age. The Son of Man will send out His angels, and they will weed out of His kingdom everything that causes sin and all who do evil. They will throw them into the blazing furnace, where there will be weeping and gnashing of teeth. Then the righteous will shine like the sun in the kingdom of their Father. Whoever has ears, let them hear."

To summarize Jesus is going to come back and when He does, the believers are going to be separated from the non-believers. Those who stand for God will be with Him in heaven and the ones who do evil and stand for the devil will burn in hell. Jesus will send out his angels to get rid of all things not of God. Whoever hears this message needs to listen and understand that this is going to happen and they need to be prepared for when He comes back.

Another scripture to refer to is (Matt 3:12.) "His winnowing fork is in his hand, and he will clear his threshing floor and gather his wheat into the barn but the chaff he will burn with unquenchable fire." This scripture is talking about how God will gather His people but he will send the ones that are not His people to hell. The wheat represents his children He will bring into his kingdom. The chaff represents wicked people who will burn in hell.

An additional scripture to look at is (Heb 4:11-13.) "Let us, therefore, make every effort to enter that rest, so that no one will perish by following their example of disobedience. For the word of God is alive and active. Sharper than any double-edged sword, it penetrates even to dividing soul and spirit, joints and marrow; it judges the thoughts and attitudes of the heart. Nothing in all creation is hidden from God's sight. Everything is uncovered and laid bare before the eyes of him to whom we must give account."

This scripture is telling you that you are accountable by the course of actions that you choose to take. You should be a living example of God, showing others Him. If you are living according to God, you can be that influence to others so that they can turn away from their worldly ways. As a child of God, you are to live like God and walk like Him. You are to be a living example of God, and how you live should make others want to know Him and have a relationship with Him. You are not only His child but you are His people and it is your job to show others and lead them to God. The Word of God is what you must be living to know what is acceptable in His eyes and what is not. God sees all and knows all things nothing is hidden from him. Your attitudes, actions, and thoughts should all show the world who God is. You will have to someday give an account for your actions and the way you chose to live your life. God doesn't want anyone to perish and He has entrusted you with the responsibility of spreading His Word, His love, His attributes, His attitudes, and His ways. One day everyone will see God.

A perfect example of how you should be as a believer is The Parable of the Bags of Gold.

(Matt 25:14-30) "Again, it will be like a man going on a journey, who called his servants and entrusted his wealth to them. To one he gave five bags of gold, to another two bags, and to another one bag, each according to his ability. Then he went on his journey. The man who had received five bags of gold went at once and put his money to work and gained five bags more. So also, the one with two bags of gold gained two more. But the man who had received one bag went off, dug a hole in the ground and hid his master's money.

"After a long time the master of those servants returned and settled accounts with them. The man who had received five bags of gold brought the other five. 'Master,' he said, 'you entrusted me with five bags of gold. See, I have gained five more.' "His master replied, 'Well done, good and faithful servant! You have been faithful with a few things; I will put you in charge of many things. Come and share your master's happiness!'

"The man with two bags of gold also came. 'Master,' he said, 'you entrusted me with two bags of gold; see, I have gained two more.' "His master replied, 'Well done, good and faithful servant! You have been faithful with a few things; I will put you in charge of many things. Come and share your master's happiness!'

"Then the man who had received one bag of gold came. 'Master,' he said, 'I knew that you are a hard man, harvesting where you have not sown and gathering where you have not scattered seed. So I was afraid and went out and hid your gold in the ground. See, here is what belongs to you.'

"His master replied, 'you wicked, lazy servant! So you knew that I harvest where I have not sown and gather where I have not scattered seed? Well then, you should have put my money on deposit with the bankers, so that when I returned I would have received it back with interest.

"'So take the bag of gold from him and give it to the one who has ten bags. For whoever has will be given more, and they will have an abundance. Whoever does not have, even what they have will be taken from them. And throw that worthless servant outside, into the darkness, where there will be weeping and gnashing of teeth."

The meaning behind this parable is that you are to stand for the kingdom of God. God has given you everything that you have; skills, talents, assets, and all those things should be put to good use for the good of his kingdom. Everything that you have is because they have been given to you from God. It is your responsibility to use what has been given to you and progress forward. You need to be striving forward using what you have been blessed with to help build the kingdom of God.

The Parable of the Ten Virgins

(Matt 25:1-13) "At that time the kingdom of heaven will be like ten virgins who took their lamps and went out to meet the bridegroom. Five of them were foolish and five were wise. The foolish ones took their lamps but did not take any oil with them. The wise ones, however, took oil in jars along with their lamps. The bridegroom was a long time in coming, and they all became drowsy and fell asleep. "At midnight the cry rang out: 'Here's the bridegroom! Come out to meet him!' "Then all the virgins woke up and trimmed their lamps. The foolish ones said to the wise, 'Give us some of your oil; our lamps are going out.'

"'No,' they replied, 'there may not be enough for both us and you. Instead, go to those who sell oil and buy some for yourselves.' "But while they were on their way to buy the oil, the bridegroom arrived. The virgins who were ready went in with him to the wedding banquet. And the door was shut. "Later the others also came. 'Lord, Lord,' they said, 'open the door for us!' "But he replied, 'Truly I tell you, I don't know you.' "Therefore keep watch, because you do not know the day or the hour.

This parable is telling you that you must be ready and prepared for when Jesus comes back. You don't know the day or the hour but need to be ready. While you are on earth, you should be doing all that you can to follow and live and walk in Jesus's ways. Each day you should lead others to Him by your behavior and your actions. Those who are not following and living according to Jesus will try to come to Him but the chance will be gone. You have to live each and every single day as if He is coming on that day. As a believer you can't just say that you believe; you have to actually live and show that Christ is in you. You must hold on to His ways and hold steadfast in knowing and trusting Him through all of your trials and tribulations before He returns.

The Sheep and the Goats

"When the Son of Man comes in his glory, and all the angels with him, he will sit on his glorious throne. All the nations will be gathered before him, and he will separate the people one from another as a shepherd separates the sheep from the goats. He will put the sheep on his right and the goats on his left.

"Then the King will say to those on his right, 'Come, you who are blessed by my Father; take your inheritance, the kingdom prepared for you since the creation of the world. For I was hungry and you gave me something to eat, I was thirsty and you gave me something to drink, I was a stranger and you invited me in, I needed clothes and you clothed me, I was sick and you looked after me, I was in prison and you came to visit me.'

"Then the righteous will answer him, 'Lord, when did we see you hungry and feed you, or thirsty and give you something to drink? When did we see you a stranger and invite you in, or needing clothes and clothe you? When did we see you sick or in prison and go to visit you?'

"The King will reply, 'Truly I tell you, whatever you did for one of the least of these brothers and sisters of mine, you did for me.' "Then he will say to those on his left,

'Depart from me, you who are cursed, into the eternal fire prepared for the devil and his angels. For I was hungry and you gave me nothing to eat, I was thirsty and you gave me nothing to drink, I was a stranger and you did not invite me in, I needed clothes and you did not clothe me, I was sick and in prison and you did not look after me.' "They also will answer, 'Lord, when did we see you hungry or thirsty or a stranger or needing clothes or sick or in prison, and did not help you?' "He will reply, 'Truly I tell you, whatever you did not do for one of the least of these, you did not do for me.' "Then they will go away to eternal punishment, but the righteous to eternal life."

This parable is talking about the ones that are God's people and the ones that aren't. When someone is one of God's chosen people, they will follow and have a close relationship with Jesus and they will have His attributes and show kindness; and love and all the attributes that He has. Those who are of God do the things that are pleasing to God and the things that bring glory to His name. The person who is not a believer lives differently. They are not following Jesus. Even if they are doing things that would be pleasing to God it is not for the right reasons. Their hearts are not right with God. The children of God are the sheep and the goats are the ones who don't follow God's way.

The sheep are the followers of Jesus and they follow His way. You should treat every single person as if they are Jesus. The goats do not do this. They do not follow Jesus's way of living. The followers of Jesus will be good to others because that is being good to Him. The goats are selfish and do not care for others they do not reflect any of the ways of Jesus. The parable is showing how Jesus will separate the ones who follow Him from the ones who don't. Followers of Jesus will reflect and show the way that He is and the way He lives. The ones who do not follow Jesus will not show His ways or who He is. (Prov. 10:17) "Whoever heeds discipline shows the way to life, but whoever ignores correction leads others astray."

CHAPTER 4

Occupied Mind

One concern that occupies some men's mind is fear. Some men can be afraid of what will happen with their lives. They are not knowing and trusting in Gods Sovereignty. Some men treat God as if He did not deliver His son for them to save them. Through Jesus you can do all things. Some Men can be concerned with their security. The security of their family, of their lives is what they may fear the most. Some men allow their circumstances to determine how they think things will be instead of trusting in God to provide. Some men are discontent and fearful of what will happen to them.

(Romans 8:32) Says "He who did not spare his own Son, but gave him up for us all—how will he not also, along with him, graciously give us all things?"

God gave up His own son for you there is nothing that he would not do or give to you. Through His son Jesus you have all things.

(Psalms 46:1-2) Says "God is our refuge and strength, an ever-present help in trouble. Therefore we will not fear, though the earth give way and the mountains fall into the heart of the sea,"

God is the one who provides you with what you need. He is your strength and your refuge in times of trouble. You have no reason to fear because He will be all that you need to overcome whatever you are facing. No matter what you are facing and how things look is not what your focus should be. It should be knowing that God is all you need to overcome all things. He is your source for everything.

(Hebrews 13:5) says "Keep your lives free from the love of money and be content with what you have, because God has said, "Never will I leave you; never will I forsake you."

You have the comfort of knowing that God will never leave you or abandon you, and no matter what will be here for you. This is a promise from God and a reminder for you that He will not leave you or abandon you in your times of trouble.

(Joshua 1:9) tells us "Be strong and courageous; do not be frightened or dismayed, for the Lord your God is with you wherever you go."

It doesn't matter where you go or what is going on, God is always with you. You have the comfort and blessing of knowing that He is always with you. So no matter what is happening or how you may feel you are never alone. You should be strong and courageous knowing that you're Lord and our God is standing with you no matter what the situation or circumstance is that you are facing. God is your strength and He is your courage to keep us strong and also brave in tough times.

Another concern that occupies some men's thoughts is lust. Some men give in to the little things that keep them from being godly men. They might have problems pornography which causes them to not keep their eyes and thoughts from impure things. To many men it may seem harmless or not a big deal but the smallest thing can set you apart from the path that God has for you. Just a small action can put your mind and heart on something that keeps you from all that God has for you. Men need to follow the word of God, allowing it to guide and direct them on the right path and to know and understand how to truly be a man of God.

(Matthew 5:27-30)

"You have heard that it was said, 'You shall not commit adultery.' But I tell you that anyone who looks at a woman lustfully has already committed adultery with her in his heart. If your right eye causes you to stumble, gouge it out and throw it away. It is better for you to lose one part of your body than for your whole body to be thrown into hell. And if your right hand causes you to stumble, cut it off and throw it away. It is better for you to lose one part of your body than for your whole body to go into hell."

The meaning of this scripture is that if you think of committing a sin, then in your heart you have already committed it. This scripture also means if something you are looking at is impure you should stop doing it. Anything that is causing you to stumble needs to be cut out and instead focus on Jesus and all that He has for you. Men should discipline themselves with Jesus's help to avoid behaviors that are not of Him and to turn away from those things becoming the men of God that they are called to be.

(1 Corinthians 6:18) Says "Flee from sexual immorality. All other sins a person commits are outside the body, but whoever sins sexually, sins against their own body."

This is very important for men to understand. Sexual immorality is committed against your own body because the Holy Spirit dwells within your body. Committing this sin is a direct spiritual attack on the sanctity of the body. You belong to God, your mind, body, heart, and soul. Your body is not your own; it is God's, and He paid the price of His Son for you. He will not take only part of you; He is going to take all of you, and that includes your body. To submit to God it has to be all of you complete devotion and obedience to him. Your body was given so that you may show the beauty of Christ. Jesus's beauty is that of love and sacrifice not concerned with appearance. You are to show through your actions that Jesus is living in you and so that others in the world may come to know and see who He is through you.

"Finally, brethren, whatever things are true, whatever things are noble, whatever things are just, whatever things are pure, whatever things are lovely, whatever things are of good report, if there is any virtue and if there is anything praiseworthy – meditate on these things" (Phil. 4:8).

This bible verse shows the kind of mindset that you should have. These are the kinds of thoughts and ideas that God wants you to dwell on. He wants you to think on the things of heaven. He wants us to be thinking about things that are good and praise-worthy. Thinking on these things and keeping your mind on these kinds of things is what will help you to focus and not be distracted by the things of the world which are all the things not of God. It's very important to keep your mind set on the things of God because thoughts can lead to actions. The wrong thoughts can lead to sinful actions.

Proverbs 5:8: "Do not go near the door of her house."

This verse is referring to men avoiding places and situations that they know are going to lead them down the wrong path. When men end up in compromising situations, they need to run completely away from them. If you run from the situation, you will be saved. Allowing bad situations to happen is not only spiritual death but not showing love to the Lord Jesus. You need to avoid and turn away from sin respecting and honoring that He gave his life for you. If you are struggling or dealing with temptation, Jesus understands because He was tempted too. Call on Jesus and He will answer; ask for His help and He will be there.

Anger can also sometimes occupy a man's mind. Some men tend to have anger towards others not realizing that God is sending them these people in their lives for a reason. God teaches you to love people who are imperfect. Some men fail to realize that they themselves have flaws and should not expect perfection from others. God sends imperfect people so that you can be set apart. God sends you imperfect people to show you what love is. God wants to magnify and show His mercy and grace through us.

"Let all bitterness, wrath, anger, clamor, and evil speaking be put away from you, with all malice" (Eph. 4:31).

This explains all the things that you are not to be. These characteristics are not Christ like and do not show who God is. You are to be a reflection of Him and all that He is to the world so they may come to know Him.

(Romans 12:10,) "Be kindly affectionate to one another with brotherly love, in honor giving preference to one another."

This explains how you should give preference to one another. You should be kind and loving to one another in order for others to see how they should be. You should look to Jesus as your role model to show how you are to be towards others. He was a servant to others and that is how you should be. Jesus put others before He put himself and this how you should be by putting others before yourself.

(Matthew 6:14)

"For if you forgive other people when they sin against you, your heavenly Father will also forgive you."

This means as you forgive others who do wrong to you, then your heavenly Father will forgive you. If you don't forgive others, then your heavenly Father will not forgive you. When you don't forgive you hold onto bitterness that will eat you up inside. Forgiveness allows you to move on and to not seek revenge for the wrong done to you.

Passive Male Syndrome can fill a man's mind. What that means is a man is not stepping into his role as a man. He is not taking the leadership role to spiritually lead his wife. He is not encouraging and uplifting his wife. He is not controlling his children. He is not willing to die for anything, meaning he doesn't value anything enough in his life that he is willing to give things up and sacrifice for it and give his all. He places other things over the things that really matter. He is not stepping up as a man and taking his place as the man God has called him to be, in order to serve the purpose that God has for him.

(Ephesians 5:25-27)

"Husbands, love your wives, just as Christ loved the church and gave himself up for her to make her holy, cleansing her by the washing with water through the word, and to present her to himself as a radiant church, without stain or wrinkle or any other blemish, but holy and blameless."

Husbands should be willing to sacrifice their life as Jesus did for the church. Husbands should show love such: as providing for her, to support her, defending her, and willing to sacrifice his life for her. Also, husbands should love as Jesus did for the church. The husband's love for his wife should be persevering no matter her imperfections and failures. A husband is accountable to help his wife further her faith and help her to become wise and holy In Jesus. In marriage it's important to make the love that Jesus had for his church the model on which your marriage is based.

Something else that some men fill their minds with is money. Some men are sometimes looking for that big promotion; or that bigger paycheck. They try to get a better job in order to be more successful to be able to buy things because they think the possessions that they own will bring them happiness.

(Matthew 6:24) "No one can serve two masters, for either he will hate the one and love the other, or he will be devoted to the one and despise the other. You cannot serve God and money.

This bible verse is saying that you cannot be all about God and all about money. You are either all about God or you are all about trying to have money. Money cannot give you all that you desire and all that you need, but God can.

1 Timothy 6:10 "For the love of money is the root of all evil: which while some coveted after, they have erred from the faith, and pierced themselves through with many sorrows."

This bible verse means the love of money can lead to other sins. This is why it is the root of all evil. The love of money can cause you not to have a close walk with God. The love of money can lead you to buy things or indulge in the other sins that cause you not to be as close with God because it's choosing to partake in things of the world instead of the things of God.

Philippians 4:19 "But my God shall supply all your need according to his riches in glory by Christ Jesus.

This bible verse means that God supplies all your needs. God has all that you need in great abundance through Jesus.

The final concern that some men allow their minds to be filled with is self-sufficiency. Men sometimes feel that they can do it all on their own. They may not like to admit they need help from God. They can allow pride to keep them from having a close relationship with God. They may not feel the need to humble themselves and fall to their knees calling out for help when they need something. You were not created to be self-sufficient. You were created to be dependent to come to God with your every need. He can provide for you things beyond this world that you can give yourself things that only come from Him. He can give you peace, He can give you strength like no other, and He can fill us with His love that makes you feel complete. God can give you each and everything that you need. He can help you through any situation. He always makes a way out even when there seems to be no way.

Proverbs 29:23

"One's pride will bring him low, but he who is lowly in spirit will obtain honor."

This means that your pride will bring you down but the one who is humble will obtain honor. You have to be careful to not think too highly of yourself, remembering that you did not create yourself but that you have a Creator who loved you enough to make you and that He has given you a purpose. You need God for everything; apart from Him you can do nothing.

Proverbs 19:21 "Many are the plans in a person's heart, but it is the Lord's purpose that prevails."

This means no matter what plans you may have in your heart that God's purpose is the one that is going to win.

You can have plans for yourself but God is the one that has his stamp of approval over what happens or doesn't happen to you.

Psalm 121:1-2 "I lift up my eyes to the mountains—where does my help come from?

My help comes from the Lord, the Maker of heaven and earth."

This means that God is where your help comes from. When you are in distress or hurting or going through trying times, He is right there with you, and He is the one lifting you up. He is the one pulling you through every situation that you go through.

CHAPTER 5

Strangulation of the Heart

What does it mean to have strangulation of the heart? It means to have the worldly ways choke out the Word of God. How does this happen? This happens when you decide to follow the world and take in the things of the world. How do you prevent your heart from strangulation? Fill yourself with the Word of God. Spend time with Him and follow His ways. In order to be filled with the love of God and for Him to fill your heart, you set yourself apart and you put Him as priority over everything in your life. When you put God first, then everything else in your life will all come together. When you fill yourself with the things of God and surrender to Him, He will change your heart.

The parable of the sower below shows an example of being rooted in the Word of God or not being rooted in the Word of God and what can happen.

The Parable of the Sower

"That same day Jesus went out of the house and sat by the lake. Such large crowds gathered around him that he got into a boat and sat in it, while all the people stood on the shore. Then he told them many things in parables, saying: "A farmer went out to sow his seed. As he was scattering the seed, some fell along the path, and the birds came and ate it up. Some fell on rocky places, where it did not have much soil. It sprang up quickly, because the soil was shallow. But when the sun came up, the plants were scorched, and they withered because they had no root. Other seed fell among thorns, which grew up and choked the plants. Still other seed fell on good soil, where it produced a crop—a hundred, sixty or thirty times what was sown. Whoever has ears, let them hear." (Matt 13: 1-9)

Below is the explanation of what this parable means.

"Listen then to what the parable of the sower means: When anyone hears the message about the kingdom and does not understand it, the evil one comes and snatches away what was sown in their heart. This is the seed sown along the path. The seed falling on rocky ground refers to someone who hears the word and at once receives it with joy. But since they have no root, they last only a short time. When trouble or persecution comes because of the word, they quickly fall away. The seed falling among the thorns refers to someone who hears the word, but the worries of this life and the deceitfulness of wealth choke the word, making it unfruitful. But the seed falling on good soil refers to someone who hears the word and understands it. This is the one who produces a crop, yielding a hundred, sixty or thirty times what was sown." (Matt 13:18-23)

This parable describes the Word of God and how everyone receives the Word of God. There are those that receive it gladly, but they are not rooted in God, so it falls away. They run when trouble comes because they are not grounded in the Word of God. Then there are those who hear the Word of God but consume themselves with the things of the world which chokes out the word. Lastly is the person who hears the Word, understanding it and applying it and producing a good crop. This person is rooted in God and in His Word that they can't be moved or deceived from the word of God they stand strong no matter what circumstance they may face in this life.

As a believer, it's very important for you to stand strong in the word of God. Being strong and grounded in the word of God protects you from being deceived against the attacks of the devil. It helps you to not allow yourself to be deceived by the world. An example is the world is very disrespectful and bashes the President not supporting him. But what does the bible say you are to do?

1 Timothy 2:1-2 "First of all, then, I urge that supplications, prayers, intercessions, and thanksgivings be made for all people, for kings and all who are in high positions,

that we may lead a peaceful and quiet life, godly and dignified in every way."

This scripture tells you that you are to be supportive of your President but the world has a different perception that is in direct conflict with God. The ways of the world are of the devil but the ways of God are in the Bible. The Bible shows how you are to handle situations of this world. For every problem that you have you have the Word of God to turn to for how to handle circumstances in this world. You are to be a reflection of God. Since you are His child you are the representation of Him in this world to show others who he is and His ways.

It is important to know and live God's word in your heart and your life.

"Blessed are those whose way is blameless, who walk in the law of the Lord! Blessed are those who keep his testimonies, who seek him with their whole heart, who also do no wrong, but walk in his ways! You have commanded your precepts to be kept diligently. Oh that my ways may be steadfast in keeping your statutes! Then I shall not be put to shame, having my eyes fixed on all your commandments. I will praise you with an upright heart, when I learn your righteous rules. I will keep your statutes; do not utterly forsake me! (Psalm 119:1-8)

Keeping the Word of God and obeying His commandments will make you blessed and blameless before Him. Your number one priority should be that you are living and walking in the ways of The Lord and doing all you can according to his Word to live an obedient life. Your joy and happiness should be found in doing the things that make The Lord happy, knowing that He is well pleased with you.

Another reason that you should know the word of God and live by it is that the Bible not only instructs you and teaches you it also tells of prophetic things to be mindful and watchful for. The book of Revelations is the perfect example of this. In Revelations it talks about the things that will happen in this world and that Jesus is coming back. As a believer, it's important to be aware of the signs and wonders and be prepared for Jesus coming back. The BIBLE stands for basic instruction before leaving Earth. Everything in the Bible is preparing you and showing you how to live and all that you need in this world before The Lord comes back for you.

Living by the word of God, meditating and focusing on the word of God, and carrying Him and His word in your heart allows you to grow more in Him. The more you are filled with His Word the more you are filled with Him. John 1:1 says "In the beginning was the Word, and the Word was with God, and the Word was God." So when you read the Bible and apply it you are filling yourself up with God. The more you fill yourself up with God the less you become like you and the more you become Like Him. You should be striving after Him and all that He is so you can become who He has called you to be in this world.

There are multiple ways to get God's Word into your heart. Here are a few below:

The first way is by making time to receive God's Word. You should prioritize and set aside time to read and take his Word into your heart, not only to understand it but to apply it to our life. When you read the Word of God concentrate on the message He is sharing. Take the time to understand what it means. Read the Word of God out loud hearing it out loud lets you see the Word of God and hearing the Word of God builds your faith. Write God's word. Writing God's Word helps His words stay in your brain. Singing God's Word is also another way of knowing His word. Sometimes the songs even help remind you of who He is and all that He does in troubled times for you.

A person that is choked out by the ways of the world is very different than someone who is walking and following the ways of God. A person that is choked out by the ways of the world does not make God a priority. They are someone who listens to what world says instead of listening to what God says. They follow the ways of the world instead of the ways of God

People who are walking in the ways of the world don't stand strong in God and in His Word. When they come up against struggles and circumstances, they allow those to define how they react. They are more concerned with what people think of them instead of being more consumed with what God thinks about them.

For anyone who is living in the ways of the world there are questions they need to ask themselves. Who are you living for? Who are you following? Do you want more out of your life than where you are now? Do you want to follow the one who made you or listen to man? Who can tell you about who you are, the one who created you or the one that was created just as you were? Following God can give you more than you can ever want or ever need. He will give you all you could ever desire. God never runs out of anything He is an abundance of many things.

You are living in a dark and fallen world. The world is full of sin and the ways of the world. People choose to listen to lies instead of believe the truth. God loves you and He created you for a purpose. You were made to have a relationship with God. Adam and Eve both sinned and that separated you from Him. God out of His mercy and His love made a plan to be able to have relationship with you. He sent His one and only son to die for you and your sins. When His son Jesus died on the cross, He suffered all the sins of the world on the cross. His son Jesus was free of sin he was perfect. He knowingly suffered for you because He loves you. Since Jesus had all the sins of the world covering Him, His father couldn't even look him that's why it says in scripture "And about the ninth hour Jesus cried out with a loud voice, saying, "Eli, Eli, lema sabachthani?" that is, "My God, my God, why have you forsaken me?" Matt (27:46) Just imagine your own father unable to look at you being completely separated from him because of sin.

Jesus because of His sacrifice made it so you are no longer an enemy of God. Jesus made it possible so that you could not only have a relationship with God but through Him have the right to be called a child of God and to call Him Father. God loved you so much that He sacrificed His Son for you because He loves you. He had a plan from the beginning that you his child would be with Him forever.

Not only do you have the gift of having a relationship with God through Jesus but you were also sent a Helper, the Holy Spirit, when you receive Jesus in your heart and repent. God equips you and supplies you with an abundance of help to handle anything that happens to you in this world. The Holy Spirit He helps to lead you in God's will for you and to have a relationship with the Son so you can know and understand God. If you know and have a close relationship with Jesus the Son of God, then you know the Father God. Jesus and God are one so to accept Jesus is to accept God. "I and the Father are one." (John 10:30) "Jesus answered: "Don't you know me, Philip, even after I have been among you such a long time? Anyone who has seen me has seen the Father. How can you say, 'Show us the Father'?" (John 14:9) These scripture tell you that if you know Jesus than you know God the Father.

It's very important for you to follow Jesus and know Him. He is your protector, your Savior; He is The Lord and God. He is the one who will help you face and overcome all the struggles in this world. If you choose to follow the ways of the world you are saying to God that you are not His child. There are only two temperatures with God: you are either hot or you are cold. If you are hot you are on fire for God doing all you can to follow Him. If you are cold then you are not following Him and are doing the things that are against Him. You are either for God or you are against Him. God says he will spit out those that are lukewarm. "So I will spit you out of my mouth, because you are only warm and not hot or cold." (Revelations 3:16)

God has given you free will. He is not going to force you to do anything because he is not a dictator. You have a choice whether you want what He wants for you or you want to go about things your own way. You have a choice of either choosing heaven or choosing hell. Choosing heaven, you not only accept Jesus but you follow Him and His ways. If you choose hell you choose to follow the ways of the world, you reject Jesus, and you don't live the life that was intended for you when you were created. There is no in between on what you choose; you are either for what is good and what is right or you are for darkness and what is evil and wrong.

The day is coming When Jesus comes back and when He does He is only going to come back for his people. The ones who are not following and walking with Jesus and haven't accepted Him will be left behind. When Jesus comes back for His people, they will be taken with him in the sky. "After that, we who are still alive and are left will be caught up together with them in the clouds to meet the Lord in the air. And so we will be with the Lord forever." (Thessalonians 4:17) All people that are left behind will feel His wrath on the earth.

"See, the Lord is coming out of his dwelling
to punish the people of the earth for their sins.
The earth will disclose the blood shed on it;
the earth will conceal its slain no longer."(Isaiah 26:21)

There will be pain and suffering and misery where people will want to die but they will not be able to. "During those days people will seek death but will not find it; they will long to die, but death will elude them." (Revelations 9:6) You are living in the end times and the best choice you can make is to choose Jesus and let Him change your life and be who He created you to be. "Repent for the kingdom of heaven is at hand." (Matthew 3:2)

CHAPTER 6

Overcoming senses of failure

How do you overcome failures? You overcome your failures through Jesus. Victory doesn't come from yourself but it comes through Jesus. God turns your failures into success.

Deuteronomy 31:6, 8 says "Be strong and bold; have no fear or dread of them, because it is the Lord your God who goes before you. He will be with you; he will not fail you or forsake you. Do not fear or be dismayed."

You do not have to fear or be afraid of failure. God will not fail you He is with you in all that you do in all that you face and in all the challenges and struggles that you overcome. Your confidence should be in Him and all that he is.

There are many examples in the Bible of people who went through failures and God turned those around for them. One example is Peter. Peter failed to have faith in

Jesus. Jesus didn't abandon Peter though. He reached out His hand and saved him. That is what God does with all of you and your failures.

"Lord, if it's you," Peter replied, "tell me to come to you on the water." "Come," He said.

Then Peter got down out of the boat, walked on the water and came toward Jesus. But when he saw the wind, he was afraid and, beginning to sink, cried out, "Lord, save me!"

Immediately Jesus reached out his hand and caught him. "You of little faith," he said, "Why did you doubt?" And when they climbed into the boat, the wind died down. Then those who were in the boat worshiped him, saying, "Truly you are the Son of God." (Matthew 14:28-32)

Another example of failure is Paul. Below are the things he did and how God turned those around for him.

(Acts 22:1-5)

"Brothers and fathers, listen now to my defense." When they heard him speak to them in Aramaic, they became very quiet. Then Paul said: "I am a Jew, born in Tarsus of Cilicia, but brought up in this city. I studied under Gamaliel and was thoroughly trained in the law of our ancestors. I was just as zealous for God as any of you are today. I persecuted the followers of this Way to their death, arresting both men and women and throwing them into prison, as the high priest and all the Council can themselves testify. I even obtained letters from them to their associates in Damascus, and went there to bring these people as prisoners to Jerusalem to be punished.

Paul shared with others what he had done in order to show the power of Jesus and how he can change you and change your life."

(Acts 22:6-16)

"About noon as I came near Damascus, suddenly a bright light from heaven flashed around me. I fell to the ground and heard a voice say to me, 'Saul! Saul! Why do you persecute me?'" 'Who are you, Lord?' I asked. 'I am Jesus of Nazareth, whom you are persecuting,' he replied. My companions saw the light, but they did not understand the voice of him who was speaking to me. "'What shall I do, Lord?' I asked. "'Get up,' the Lord said, 'and go into Damascus. There you will be told all that you have been assigned to do.' My companions led me by the hand into Damascus, because the brilliance of the light had blinded me. "A man named Ananias came to see me. He was a devout observer of the law and highly respected by all the Jews living there. He stood beside me and said, 'Brother Saul, receive your sight!' And at that very moment I was able to see him. "Then he said: 'The God of our ancestors has chosen you to know his will and to see the Righteous One and to hear words from his mouth. You will be his witness to all people of what you have seen and heard. And now what are you waiting for? Get up, be baptized and wash your sins away, calling on his name."

Even after Paul had persecuted Christians and came against God, he was given His mercy having his sight restored. Not only did he have his sight restored but he was chosen to do God's will and told what he was to do. Even though he had sinned and had messed up he was still able to be saved and able to be used. You can be uplifted and encouraged even when you fail. God still loves you and can help you to do great things in spite of your failures.

Romans 3:23 says "For all have sinned and fallen short of the glory of God." This verse is encouraging by letting you know that we all have sinned and fallen short of the glory of God. You have to understand that you are not perfect and it is only through Jesus that you can be all that God wants you to be. Where you have imperfections and fall short God provides and makes up for what you lack.

There are two failures. One failure is feeling you are not pleasing God and measuring up to what He wants you to do and to be. His word reminds you that even if you fail He has unconditional love for you. John 3:16 says "For God so loved the world that he gave His one and only Son, that whoever believes in Him shall not perish but have eternal life. "This verse reminds you that God's love is unconditional. There is nothing He would not do for you. He gave His one and only son because He loved you so much that He wanted to make sure you could have a relationship with Him. He wants you to be with Him forever. There is no end to how much God loves you. You don't need to feel like a failure because through Jesus you are victorious in all that God has and wants for you. Even when you fall short and feel you don't measure up, God loves you, and because the blood of His Son Jesus covering you, He sees you as perfect even if you don't view yourself that way.

Another form of failure is when you try to accomplish something and it doesn't work out. This could be a failed relationship, friendship, marriage, job, or personal goal. Here is a scripture that you can be reminded of when it comes to failures that you may face. Psalm 73:26 says "My flesh and my heart may fail, but God is the strength of my heart and my portion forever." This verse reminds you that even if you fail, God is your strength. When you put your trust in God whenever things are not going well or you are going through tough times, He is our portion forever. The more you trust in Him the better things turn out even when things go wrong because you know that you are in His hands. God has all that you need and can provide you with all things. He wants you to lean on Him and trust in Him with everything in your life.

One thing that you must know and understand is that it's not about the setbacks or the failures that you have. It is important to realize your perspective in whatever you face in this world is what counts. "I have told you these things, so that in me you may have peace. In this world you will have trouble. But take heart! I have overcome the world."(John 16:33) This verse is a very good reminder for you. Through God you have peace. You are going to have problems and obstacles and things that you will have to face but you have the comfort that you will never face them alone. God has already overcome the world, and because He is with you, you can be sure he will guide you and show you exactly how you can also overcome the world. Even when you fail, you don't because you have God through the Lord Jesus. Through Jesus you can have anything you need.

If you are sad and feeling at unease, God is right there with you to comfort you and make you feel calm and at peace. If you are feeling lonely he can fill you up with his love. It's important to understand that when you stop placing your needs and your wants and desires on things of this world and start realizing all that you have is in God through Jesus, He can make all of your dreams come true. What He has planned for you is the very best, more than you can possibly imagine.

Another reason that you may deal with failure is you try to do it all on your own. (John 5:15) says "I am the vine; you are the branches. If you remain in me and I in you, you will bear much fruit; apart from me you can do nothing. This verse tells you that apart from God you can do nothing. When you try to go about things on our own, you will not succeed. Sometimes the things that you want to do are not what God wants for you and He will allow something not to go the way you think it should go. An example is a relationship. You may really love someone and they are not right for you and you continue to be with that person but in the end it doesn't work out. God saves you from future pain he saves you from the things that are not good for you. He saves you from all the things that are not best for you. He always works on your behalf for you to have the very best. He doesn't want you to settle for less than you deserve. Part of that is understanding who you are, that you are a child of the most high King.

When you begin to understand who you are and who you belong to, then you can change your perception of what you consider makes you valuable. (Colossians 2:10) says "And in Christ you have been brought to fullness. He is the head over every power and authority. This means that you are complete in Jesus and that He has all power and authority. All that you are is defined by Jesus and all that you are meant to be is in Him. You don't have to worry or fear when things are not in your control because He is in control even when you have failures.

You have the comfort of knowing that you are not defined by this world or our failures but you are defined by who you are in Jesus. He is your Lord and your Creator and can help you to become all the things that He made you to be. You have the victory in all things because you have Jesus and He is the one who knows exactly what you need and what you should have and He knows exactly how to overcome all things. You are not defined by your failures at all. It's not how many times you fall but how many times do you get back up again and how you react and respond to your failures. Jesus will help you to stand strong. No matter how many times you fall in life He will lift you back up again and He will never let you down. God keeps all His promises and He is relentless in his love for you. He will fight on your behalf no matter what comes against you and will always be there when you feel that you can't go anymore. Jesus will be your strength. Just call on him and trust in Him in the circumstances that you face.

The last thing to understand is that sometimes God allows you to fail to make you push harder. God knows your true potential and all that you are to be in Him. The challenges and failures cause you to change and cause you to become who God created you to be. If you didn't sometimes face challenges, then you wouldn't know what you are capable of in God. Challenges force you to grow even when you fail. When things are too easy for you it doesn't allow you to be molded and shaped the way that God wants you to be. Whether you realize it or not even your struggles and your failures have a purpose behind them.

CHAPTER 7

Believing (God never fails)

O ne of the most important things in being a child of God is your faith in Him. Do you believe that He will do what He says he will do? Do you believe that even in hardships He is working everything out?.

Joshua 21:45

"Not one of all the Lord's good promises to Israel failed; everyone was fulfilled."

This scripture reminds us that God does not break promises. He will fulfill each and every single promise because his words are pure and true.

Here is another scripture to help you remember that God never fails.

Psalm 33:4

"For the word of the Lord is right and true; he is faithful in all he does."

This reaffirms that God's words are always right and true. He only tells the truth in His word. In all that He does He is faithful. You never have to worry about the intentions and motives that God has for you because all that He has for you is good.

Below is an example of a scripture showing what God wants for you.

Jeremiah 29:11 "'For I Know The Plans I Have For You' Declares the Lord, 'Plans to Prosper You and Not to Harm You, Plans to Give You Hope and a Future.'"

This tells you that God has plans that are good for you and that will give you a hope and a future. By knowing and embedding in your hearts that He wants the best for you so you can know that you are safe in His loving arms. You can trust Him and rely on Him, knowing that He will always be there.

There are plenty of examples in the bible of people who believed that God would fail them. The example that I will use is the story of Sarah.

Genesis 16:2 so she said to Abram, "The LORD has kept me from having children. Go, sleep with my slave; perhaps I can build a family through her." Abram agreed to what Sarai said.

Sarah and Abraham decided together instead of waiting for God to bless them with a child that they would do things their own way. Because they chose to go about things their own way and not believe that God would give them what He promised they had to suffer the consequences.

Genesis 16:3-4 says "Then Sarai, Abram's wife, took Hagar her maid, the Egyptian, and gave her to her husband Abram to be his wife, after Abram had dwelt ten years in the land of Canaan. So he went in to Hagar, and she conceived. And when she saw that she had conceived, her mistress became despised in her eyes."

This scripture points out that because of Abraham and Sarah's choice to conceive through the maid Hagar it caused friction after she had finally conceived. Since Hagar conceived and Sarah couldn't, it caused her to feel like she was superior to Sarah.

Below is another consequence of the choice that Sarah and Abraham made.

Genesis 16:5 says "Then Sarai said to Abram, "My wrong be upon you! I gave my maid into your embrace; and when she saw that she had conceived, I became despised in her eyes. The Lord judge between you and me."

Sarah is feeling the weight of the decision that she made with Abraham and blaming him for what she told him to do. She felt that it was his fault for her listening to her instead of telling her no because now she was despised by the servant who conceived.

Yet another consequence of the choice that made is described in the verse below.

Genesis 16:6 says "So Abram said to Sarai, "Indeed your maid is in your hand; do to her as you please." And when Sarai dealt harshly with her, she fled from her presence."

This verse is describing Sarah telling her husband to do what he wants with the maid. She is also angry and bitter because the maid was able to conceive a child and she could not so she resented her for it.

There were many consequences of Abraham and Sarah trying to do things their own way but God did not break his promise to them. Below is God fulfilling the promise that he had made to Sarah and Abraham.

Genesis 21:2,: "For Sarah conceived, and bare Abraham a son in his old age, at the set time of which God had spoken to him."

God kept his promise that he had spoken of to Abraham and Sarah even though they were impatient. They went about things in their own way but it did not change the promise that God made to them. Even when you do things your own way and make mistakes, God always makes a way to keep His promises. You may fail God but He will never fail you. God is a faithful God who does what He says that He will do.

There are many scriptures of God's promises and how He never fails. He always comes through just as He says that he will. Below is him speaking to the Israelites and all He has done for them.

Deuteronomy 2:7

"The Lord your God has blessed you in all the work of your hands. He has watched over your journey through this vast wilderness. These forty years the Lord your God has been with you, and you have not lacked anything."

God is telling his people the Israelites how He has blessed them in the work of their hands. He has watched over them through their journey. He was with them and provided and gave them all they needed.

When you begin to know and understand who God is, then you can truly know and understand that God never fails. He is the same God who used Moses to free His people. The same God who made it so Sarah could bear a child even in old age. The same God who delivered David out of all of his sins, even making him a king. The same God who used Paul for good even though he was killing Christians and was against Him.

There are no limits to what God can do. He can use anyone anywhere for the purpose He has for them. He can perform miracles. The one thing that you need to know and always remember is that no matter what, God will never fail you. His plan will always happen one way or another. His promises always come to pass. He does not break his promises; He does not go back on His word. He will never change He is the same today as He will be tomorrow and the next day. You never have to worry or stress about relying or depending on God. You never have to think twice about how He will treat you in your circumstance. He is a fair God and always does what is right.

Below is another scripture that you need to remember no matter what you face.

Hebrews 13:5 "Keep your lives free from the love of money and be content with what you have, because God has said, "Never will I leave you; never will I forsake you." God is saying he will never leave or forsake you. When you remember this, it should be a comfort to us, because no matter what you face or go through He will be right there through it all. Even when it seems as if God is far away or not close to you, He is with you. It's important that you believe in Him no matter how you feel.

Why do people believe God fails? Unrealistic or faulty expectations. There is nothing that God cannot do. Nothing is impossible for God. Sometimes what you want or expect of God is not realistic for what He wants for you.

He wants more than you can imagine but sometimes that does not line up or match with what you want for yourself.

There are tragedies and bad things that happen in your life that seem unfair but what does God tells you about that? Matthew 5:45 says "That you may be children of your Father in heaven. He causes his sun to rise on the evil and the good, and sends rain on the righteous and the unrighteous."

So what does this scripture mean? It means that bad things don't just happen to bad people but also to good people. Some would say that it is unfair, but you must understand that everything that God allows to happen is for a reason. Romans 8:28 says "And we know that in all things God works for the good of those who love him, who have been called according to his purpose." God is working on your behalf and doing what is good for you. Even when you don't think so or see what He is doing, you need to know that He is for you even when things go wrong. God deserves all the glory and all the honor and all the praise for who He is and all that He does.

Another reason that people believe that God will fail is that they are listening to the world and not to God. You need to read His Word to understand who He is. The world cannot tell you who God is because the world does not know who God is. 1 John 4:8 says "Whoever does not love does not know God, because God is love."The world that we are living in is missing love so they are missing God. People are lacking compassion and sympathy.

The Word of God will help you to know who He is and understand Him. It's important for you to know God so you can understand what He is capable of. If you know God, then you know that He is capable of everything and that apart from him you can do nothing. Remember to put your trust in God. Do not put your trust in yourself or in man. No one knows you better than your Creator; He knows what is best for you. You cannot put your trust in yourself because you will fail every time. You can do nothing apart from God. He is your source of everything. Whether you know or realize it or not, He has a hand in all things that happen. He is in control not you. God allows certain things to work in your favor or not, and if He ends up telling you no on something it is because He always has a greater plan and purpose for you.

Another reason people believe God will fail them is that they are being deceived. There is a false idea that God is angry and wants to punish you, but that is a lie. He does not want to punish you but he will allow certain things to happen to you to guide you on the right path because he only wants what is best for you. God is more than you can conceive. The one thing that you should always remember is that God is good. When he created the world, he made it for all you. He made it so you could have water. He made it so you could have food. He has always provided everything you have. God does not like sin because it is not of him. Sin causes a separation from Him, but His Son Jesus has made it so that we can have a relationship with Him and be cleansed of all of our sins.

God wants to be with you in a beautiful world that is full of righteousness and goodness, a world free of sin, a world that has no darkness. As a child of God, you have an enemy, and his name is the devil. He wants to destroy God's children, but the devil cannot do that because no one can snatch you out of the hands of your father. Scripture says "My Father, who has given them to Me, is greater than all; and no one is able to snatch them out of the Father's hand."(John 10:29) The devil puts attacks against the children of God in the mind and against the body and the heart, but God has been so loving that He has given you spiritual weapons that protect you against the devil's attacks.

You have been given the armor of God. What is the armor of God? The armor of God is (Ephesians 6:10-18) "Finally, be strong in the Lord and in his mighty power. Put on the full armor of God, so that you can take your stand against the devil's schemes. For our struggle is not against flesh and blood, but against the rulers, against the authorities, against the powers of this dark world and against the spiritual forces of evil in the heavenly realms. Therefore put on the full armor of God, so that when the day of evil comes, you may be able to stand your ground, and after you have done everything, to stand. Stand firm then, with the belt of truth buckled around your waist, with the breastplate of righteousness in place, and with your feet fitted with the readiness that comes from the gospel of peace. In addition to all this, take up the shield of faith, with which you can extinguish all the flaming arrows of the evil one. Take the helmet of salvation and the sword of the Spirit, which is the Word of God."

The helmet assures you of your salvation. God clothes you in salvation. Putting on the helmet of salvation protects you from attacks from the devil or from doubts about our salvation and him putting thoughts in our minds that try to separate us from God. Another piece of armor is the breast plate of righteousness; this is to obey God's commandments and live in a way that is honorable to him. Putting this on protects you from the devil launching attacks that can cause you to fall into sin. The next piece of armor is the belt of truth; this is knowing God's truth. Putting on the belt of truth protects against the lies and deceptions of the enemy. The next piece of armor is the shield of faith. This is your hope in God. It's important because it protects you against the lies of the devil and the way he tries to discourage you to have doubt and not believe. The next piece of armor is your feet that are shod with the gospel of peace. This armor is spreading the news of the gospel and the peace of God to others but also standing firm in the gospel and having the peace of God, knowing no matter what you face God is in control of all things. If you are not fitted with the gospel of peace, then the devil can cause you to slip from your foundation and you will lose your peace. The last piece of armor is the sword of the spirit. This is the Word of God and it's important so that the enemy cannot tell you lies that lead you astray from God. Knowing and understanding the Word of God helps you to stand strong especially against the lies of the devil and the attacks he launches. You have to know Gods promises and truths in His Word to come against the lies and tricks of the devil that come your way. If you keep Gods Word in your heart than if you see or hear lies from the devil you can block them with Gods truth that will give you hope and peace.

Another weapon God has given you is the ability to say prayers to him. Your prayers to God help you fight against the attacks of the devil not just for yourselves but also for others. As you begin to pray for others God breaks the chains over them. Another weapon that you have against the attacks of the enemy is the ability to speak in tongues. It is a gift from God to speak in his heavenly language that communicates directly with him. With this language you are able to praise God speaking in tongues or singing in tongues. Praise is also a weapon against the devil. The more that you believe in God and what He will do the more that you will begin to see all that he will do and all he has for you.

So why should you believe that God will not fail you? Because for one thing he is faithful. God does not give up on you. He does not walk away nor he does not think less of you when you fail. He uses your failures and turns them into successes. Even when you make mistakes, He is still working things out for your good.

Another reason you should believe He will not fail you is his grace. God blesses you even when you do nothing to deserve to be blessed. He is always doing things for you and blessing you in your life whether you realize it or not. The perfect example of his grace is your salvation. You did nothing at all to deserve salvation to be able to go to heaven. It is only because of His grace that made it possible for you to have salvation.

Another reason you should believe God will never fail is because of His mercy. God has constant mercy for you and your circumstances. He hears your every cry when you call out to him. God feels your pain and your struggles. He is with you and literally feels all that you feel He is right there with you through it all. He will never leave or forsake you no matter what you face. You can overcome the world because he has already overcome the world. God feels more than you can ever possibly imagine. He is an extremely merciful God. He sees his child hurting and He does all He can to strengthen you and push you forward in order to grow and become all that He has called you to be.

Another reason you should believe God will never fail is because of His love. God is love and if you know love you know God. God's love never runs out for you. His love is everlasting and He loves you unconditionally. He does not love any one of us more than another. Galatians 3:28,"There is neither Jew nor Gentile, neither slave nor free, nor is there male and female, for you are all one in Christ Jesus."There is nothing that God would not do for you. God does not want to be separated from you. He wants to spend time with you He wants to help you. He wants to completely surround you with His love. He is constantly full of love for you. He wants to rescue you when you need help. All you have to do is ask. He wants to lift you up when you feel weak when you feel like you cannot go any longer. There is nothing that God would not do for you.

Another reason you should believe God will never fail is because He has all that you need. If He has all that you need, then you should know He will not fail you. God is your provider. If you need food He provides. If you need shelter, He provides. If you need comfort, He provides. If you feel alone, He surrounds you. If you are sad, He lifts you up. If you are weak, He gives us strength. If you feel lost He helps you find your way back to Him. Sometimes God even uses you to help others so that they can have what they need.

Below are reassuring scriptures that will fill you with hope and comfort, being assured God will not fail.

Isaiah 14:27 says "For the Lord Almighty has purposed, and who can thwart him? His hand is stretched out, and who can turn it back?

This bible verse is saying what God has purposed who can stop Him? His hand is stretched out, who can move is hand? God's plan for your life is unmovable. It doesn't matter who or what tries to come against His plan for you and your life it will not fail. God's plan will succeed and will be carried out.

Proverbs 21:30 says"There is no wisdom, no insight, no plan that can succeed against The LORD"

There is no one smarter than God and no one who has more insight than God. No plan in this world can succeed against the plan of God. When you know and believe that no one and nothing can prevail against the plan of God, then you have new strength in Him and peace of mind.

Everyone needs to know and understand the power of God. He has all power and all authority over everything and everyone. There is nothing that He does not know about. There is nothing that He does not see or understand. There is no limitation for God. There is nothing that He cannot do. He can do any and all things. God makes a way when there is no way. When you are in times of struggle, you must look to His Word and His promises to remind you of all that you have been given and that nothing is impossible with God.(Matt 19:26 Jesus looked at them and said, "With man this is impossible, but with God all things are possible." When you realize that it is not your standards you should be looking to it is the standard of God that you should be looking to, then you will not fail. The Word of God has an answer for the problems of this world and how to overcome them. He is the standard that you should live by. God is your resource and your lifeline. When you call out to Him, He answers. God helps you achieve what you cannot do on our own. If you can't afford something, He can provide the resources so that you can. If you do not have the skill to do something,

He can provide you in abundance with the skills to do what you need to do. If you have God in your life there is no limit to the heights you can reach in your life. He can make ways for you to do things that you have not done. See things you haven't seen. Experience things that you have not experienced. He has an abundance of everything you could ever possibly need. When it comes to failure it's not about confidence and faith in yourself but about your confidence and faith in God and what He can do through you and in you.

CHAPTER 8

Realizing the Truth

Am going to share my own personal testimony of what I have gone through and what God helped me overcome. I was living for years walking in the ways of the world. Things were not going right or working out for me. I didn't realize it at the time but I was looking for something to make me feel complete. I thought I would find it in my relationship with my boyfriend I had but I didn't. I thought if I worked that I would find purpose but I didn't. I was so filled with things of the world that I couldn't see God calling me to come back to Him, my first love. It started with Him cleansing my life and then opening my eyes to Him as He brought me back. The first thing He started with was opening my eyes to ending my relationship. The next thing was ending friendships that were not good for me. The final thing that He allowed to happen was for me to get a job. The job I had was not good for me, so I quit. When I quit, I had time to think and focus and pray. God drew me close to Him through my parents. I saw them suddenly change their ways and being on fire for God. Suddenly my heart was on fire for God. I started putting scriptures all over my wall. I felt so alive and refreshed to read the Word of God. I begin to praise and worship with my parents and I started to feel the joy and the love and the presence of God. My dad began to prophesy because of the closeness that he started to have with God. I started to have a godly jealousy and I had started to listen for God. Unfortunately, I began to be under spiritual attack. As a child of God, you have an enemy that is the devil who is constantly trying to do things to you, but God always protects you. I started to hear voices in my head. The voices in my head were deceiving me telling me things to make me feel less than I am. The voices were trying to make me feel that God was upset with me. I felt so much shame and guilt for something that didn't even happen. I was having delusions about things I thought took place. I was feeling depressed. I wasn't eating. I was feeling like I wanted to hurt myself. I was feeling weak and vulnerable but one thing I learned through it all was God was always with me. He never left my side. I went into the hospital as last resort. I was given pills and a shot. I was told that I was bipolar schizophrenic. At that time in my life, I was feeling hopeless, like I had nothing left. I thought I was going to die and go to hell. I was in the hospital for two weeks. I had doctors constantly checking on me and other patients screaming and yelling who were also under spiritual attack. After almost two weeks, I was eating again, becoming healthier and stronger but the voices were still there. I was released from the hospital and I couldn't have been happier to leave but the battle wasn't over yet. My parents took me home and were praying for me and whole churches were praying for me. I began to put scriptures everywhere. My parents got rid of anything that could cause any spirits to be in the house while I was in the hospital. Slowly but surely, God built me up teaching me to know that He was with me by growing more in Him and trusting that He was going to deliver me. Not only did God teach me to trust but He took away the bad habits and things in me that were not good. God cleansed and healed my heart of wickedness that was hurtful and mean. He took profanity out of my mouth. He changed my mind and the way I looked at things. He opened my eyes to the world I was living in. It was months after being in the hospital, but God heard my prayers and Jesus delivered me. I didn't hear the voices anymore. I was healthy and vibrant with color in my face and hope and thankfulness in my heart. I was thankful He rescued me. I was happy to be alive and okay after enduring that spiritual attack. Even to this day I am so thankful and happy He did that for me. I just want to tell everyone and share with them how loving and amazing God is. It doesn't matter what you have done, God can help you and restore you. No matter what you are facing and going through, He can give you new life. He can mold and shape you. There are many people out there who are oppressed, feeling hopeless, like there's no way out but I want it to be known Jesus is the way. If you have an incurable disease, Jesus can heal you. If you have a sickness, He can heal you. If you are hurting, He can fix you. If you feel broken, He can mend you. If you have an unclean heart, He can change you. There literally is nothing that Jesus cannot do for you. The most important thing I learned through it all was this God's love is unconditional. He loves you at your worst and at your best. He loves you always. He wants to help you and to save you. Even after that spiritual attack, I got spiritually attacked again, and you know what? Jesus delivered me. God is so faithful He does not give up on us at all. He does not forget us. He does not overlook us. God's love is so amazing and can change your whole world your whole life. He has pure true love for everyone. If you don't have a relationship with Him, its not too late. He has His arms opened wide saying come unto me. He will wrap you in His loving arms to forget all the troubles of the world. He is right there with you in the fire. He is suffering with you when you go through things. Call on His name and He will answer you. He will support you and uplift you and give you hope that you didn't know you could have.

After going through spiritual attacks and seeing how Jesus saved me and turned my perspective around, I am forever changed. I was living in sin and thinking about myself and what I wanted and what I needed, being very selfish. He changed my whole outlook on life and in this new world of mine, I will never be the same. God opened my eyes and pulled me out of the darkness into the light. I was blind but now I can truly say that I see. You need

Jesus in your life to help you change, to comfort, to take you by the hand to overcome the world.

If you are living in sin, now is the time to repent and change your ways. Jesus is coming back soon, and when He does, you want to be right with Him. What is going on right now in the world are end times. Prophecies in the bible are coming to pass. God is bringing all His people back to him but they have to turn away from their wicked ways and truly repent. There are many people who don't fully realize or understand all that they have in Jesus. Since you have Jesus you can be healed. Since you have Jesus you are saved from hell. Since you have Jesus, you have been adopted as a child of God. Through Jesus, you can pray to God and He will hear you and answer your prayers. (John 14:13-14)" And whatever you ask in my name, that I will do, that the Father may be glorified in the son. If you ask anything in my name I will do it." Jesus guides you and leads you into all the things God has planned for you. You need to lean on Jesus everyday. He is Lord of all and has all power and authority. He wants you to have a relationship with Him. He wants you to understand who you are in Him. The love God has for everyone is beyond what can be understood.

God doesn't want anyone to perish but your choices are all your own free will. You have a choice: choose to follow Jesus or to reject Him and follow the world. It is not going to be an easy walk in this world following Jesus but it will be worth it. He will never leave nor forsake you but you have to hold onto your faith and not be shaken or moved by the things of this world. He wants you to stand firm in Him and trust in Him no matter what. God's wrath is going to pour out on the earth and his children are going to be protected but those who don't know Jesus are not going to be protected. As believers right now is the time to repent and to change if you are not walking right with Jesus and walking in His ways. If you know someone who is not a child of God and doesn't know Jesus now is the time to spread the gospel. Now is the time to share the good news so they know they are loved and can be saved. People living in the world do not understand how important it is to repent and turn to Jesus, but as a believer you need to do all you can so others can hear the gospel and accept Jesus before it's too late. When Jesus returns to the earth to save His people the rapture is going to happen only once. After that there is going to be so much devastation and tragedies and disasters happening that people will want to escape it but they will not be able to.

Below I will put the sinner's prayer for anyone who has not been saved or for anyone that wants to be able to help someone to become saved. Being saved is not about just saying these words out loud and confessing them but truly believing in your heart and changing.

Pray this prayer: "Dear God, I am sorry for my sins and the life that I have lived. I need your forgiveness! I believe that your son Jesus Christ died to pay for my sins and that you raised him from the dead. I ask you, Jesus to come into my heart. I surrender my life to you completely and will follow you faithfully from now on. Thank you for giving me eternal life."

After becoming saved and becoming a believer it's important that you buy a bible to understand the Word of God in order to grow in Jesus and learn how to walk in His ways and no longer walk in the ways of the world. Jesus will help you change your sinful worldly ways and mindsets. No matter what you face in this life he will be with you at every turn.

CPSIA information can be obtained
at www.ICGtesting.com
Printed in the USA
LVHW050408140422
716185LV00009B/422